Souls of Benghazi

God Sees

Catherine Ferrier

DEDICATION

This book was birthed and written at the Eternal Flame of Hope at Oceana Naval Base in Virginia Beach, Virginia.

MIA, Killed in Action, POW, Wounded Warriors, Survivors. Are we all not the same when manipulated by atrocities in the thinking of Governments who are supposed to be put in place to be for the benefit of mankind?

Good people down for the sake of a few people's vanity and sick thinking. This book is dedicated to you. We are all alive because of you.

You are our true leaders. You know the 'Heavenly More' about Earth that we are blinded from, being in the physical form.

The veil is thinner and death is truly 'different' than in times past, I invoke you, all my forefathers, mothers, children and forces of God to unite us with the legions in Heaven and on Earth. Those of you still surviving here, we need your wisdom and expertise. I humbly ask you to speak the truth and lead at this time.

CONTENTS

INTRODUCTION

Yes, this book is a 'channeled' or 'intuited' work. When it is Catherine speaking, it is in parenthesis. The rest of the book is either researched or channeled.

Often, people come to me to speak to their loved ones who have crossed over. I did not expect this particular communication. No one asked me for it. At least no one that would normally be considered 'alive'. It came to me, loudly and clearly on its own. Indeed, I questioned its authority for 9 months because of my feelings for the current government and its movements. I put this communication through every discriminatory 'test' I could dream up because I cannot exist in ego and remain under my commitment, love and devotion to My God. I wanted to make sure that it was Divinely Guided.

Alas, the 'call' remained. Finally, one day, I intuited a message that went a little like this: "It is a Divine Triangle that comes to you. Go into the triangle. It is a Divine Union between God and Man. You will see that there are ministers that can and do work from the other side. Ty has been given the grace to be one of those Divine."

Because I do not deny my intuition, I stopped everything and spent several more months going into meditation, which then required me to cleanse and clear on many levels inside myself as I studied the wisdom from on High that was being shown to me.

Finally, I asked for one more affirmation as I realized that this needed to be written down for the world to see. It wasn't just information meant for me. It took about a week to 'hear' and 'feel' something I could not deny in my own intuition.

What I needed to do at that point was to go to the Eternal Flame of Hope and pray to release all my resistance and control. I also needed to ask permission of these fallen warriors and accept responsibility for that permission. It isn't necessary for anyone to understand that but me. In any case, I didn't waste any time. I dropped the kids off at school the next morning and headed over to the memorial. What you are about to read is birthed there. I am aware of skeptics. Can't waste my time with you. You've been around my whole life.

Once I agreed to the book, I felt that it should be called 'Talks With Ty', but am clearly instructed that its name is to be 'Souls of Benghazi' because that moment in time is where the country and the Earth took a stand against the current form of humanity and its direction. The communications are not solely with Ty. As I see him the most clearly, and hear him the most clearly, I can also see that there are many from other countries and other worlds here; all united under the direction of God and under the operating authority of the Archangels. I've often thought I've been one to receive this information at this time because I was working on my third researched and channeled book at the time called 'Walking With Angels' when 'Souls of Benghazi' was birthed.

The message of this book, or channeled information is this. Somehow, there is a building up of something in Heaven against something else. This something else is growing and must be stopped at all costs. Is it Satan? Is it Heaven vs. Hell? Feels like it to me. However, I do not get a clear image of that. What I do know is that it is very clearly a fight between right and wrong. And, what is truly not our fight has landed here anyway. We are being asked to seek refuge. We are being asked to fight, but not against people or individuals, but rather a consciousness that is 'attacking the whole of humanity' aligning one against the other to our entire destruction.

As for 'leaders' and 'politicians', in my opinion; no, in my knowing, anyone who can send in a 'drone' to watch live, then go to sleep or whatever, and make up a big story afterward is not operating in any way, shape or form under the definition of 'right'. We are foolish to allow them to be in the hired role of leadership. I would not be able to keep an employee who does that. Nor, would I be able to keep a friend or family member who does things like that. Our country must no longer keep hired employees who think and operate in such ways. In fact, no country should. It will put us at war against ourselves.

We, the United States of America, are a nation that was birthed purely, clearly and simply under God. In my opinion, our forefathers followed the commandments given to Moses in order to live 'Rightly under his name, guidance and protection".

England, under its rule, had lost itself at the time. We broke away. Our forefathers worked hard and kept their lives at risk for our future.

I need to do that same thing for my children too. Don't you?

1 TALKS WITH TY BEGIN

I am no dummy. I wasn't raised to be dumb. I was raised and trained to be smart in all endeavors. I may not have been trained for truth, but I was certainly raised in it and the vibration of it all the way around.

Do you think I and the others would have run so fiercely into battle if were not for a reason?! It was obvious to us what was going on and after we saved the people we were going to speak out about it loud and clear to our 'captain' first, then to the world. You learn things by watching, waiting and listening. If you will feel free to let me chatter here, I have been waiting for my friends to join me before speaking out completely. Yes, one of those friends waited for was Cathy. (Sorry about that). It's alright. Large space. Large job and you are not weak.

We may have been told by our superiors to stand down, but we were not stopped. The gravity and the realization of the situation spoke for itself. If we let this continue to go on in our 'secret services', we would be next. Who is against who here?!

We could hear the scatter and array of pain that was being inflicted. We could see the drones. We could see what was 'asleep' and what was not. A decision had to be made. To stand down is not an option Mr. Obama or whoever or whatever you are occupying space and time in that benign being. Yes, when you are where we were, you knew, could see, were aware of the secret forces and armies of these people, that were created out of some magnitude and cooperation of awareness. Where we stood we could see them passing by us days before the action completely happened. Tried earlier to get ambassador to leave. Weren't sure where and when strike would be, but no doubt of its planning, its existence. Couldn't get message loud and clear to him. Post was safer for him, he thought. Obviously, no one was left protecting it. Those kinds of orders only come from 'above' at the 'almighty white house'.

Days before. Days before. Half disgust, half fright for us. Our kingdom, our territory we were sent to protect no longer houses the definition of government that relies on us, it's people to do anything other than their dirty work. And, it was clear we would be next if we spoke or did anything about it. This kind of talk was not new. Been traveling in our gears for a lifetime it seems as this train wreck has hit the country. NO ONE LEFT BEHIND. Hah. Don't be fooled anymore. This is a new order.

Cathy, you constantly call him and his 'puppeteers' and cohorts greedy, impetuous snobby, spoiled rotten little self-absorbed teenagers that are drunken and have been given the keys to the only family car and so on. My love, I am here to tell you that some people are inherently bad people. Right, wrong or indifferent, that's just how it is. Supervise yourself only. We will take care of the rest. Army at heaven's side. Need you to tell the rest, tell the world that Heaven is still an army that is at our Military's side. That is why I have instructed you to add the things to this book that you've been gathering. We are not dead. Death is not the same as it used to be. The veil is closer and the tread of the tire is longer, wider and thicker than it used to be. Meaning that what you decide at death's door determines and undermines where you are lead at the beginning of your 'death door'. Mine was to be with you and write. Then write again and lead the 'ghost ship' otherwise known as 'Heaven's fleet of souls against the dammed'. (Not sure I follow you, but okay, here we go).

Now, there is not to blame. There is only to do. Free will on Earth is damaged a bit but there is still room to bloom. And bloom we will or there shan't be an Earth any more.

(I ask if others are with them that died that day). Yes, can you not feel the crowd of souls speaking with you. I am the loudest. (He laughs). Don't worry about it. Let Go Let God place his signature upon you. Rest to know you will get the job done as I always knew you would. Heroes are in the presence. (I am in the presence of heroes, you mean?)

Yes, I have collected, or rather it has been sent to me a charge over a union of heroes of old ~ POW, MIA, ACTIVE LOST and RETIRED to form the triangle from both sides of war and from all sides of the fence. Now we connect with you who are still on Earth and prepared. (Yes, that is one of my earliest memories of knowing since early childhood that I would "face Hussein". Never knew what it meant until now. Actually, I still don't know, but I'm working on it!). Good. Let's go. MOVE ON COUNTRY! War on the home front. Soon will be undermined by legions of light as a barrier against the other mights of existence.

Our teams. Our men, women and children are being trained to keep a watchful eye, yet they really are having to watch their own back. There is strife in our military, not in the direct leadership but in the bowels of the books and phone calls that are being created for them to lead from. Stupidity at the top equals stupidity at the bottom. It leaves grown men to make their own judgment calls against what is real and what is not real. After all, the battle is all around you. "Stand down", really?! And, time and time again tell me?! Tell us?! While we watch your drone in the sky still hoping, still advancing seeing that the military is there to help us all survive. Should have shot you bastards out of the sky. Dying did not come easy. Time to think. Time to plan. Desire to live twofold. Sang songs. Pride. Of a sudden I was back in my youth – that white shirt you saw me in Cathy. (I remember). Help your friends, the one who sang Christmas carols during here birthing her children. (I will call her today). She adores you. (I adore her. Why are we speaking of her?) If my death memory recall is correct, that is something like what I was doing. Took about 20 minutes or so to die, so I don't know exactly where I was during that time. Sang Star Spangled Banner, My Country Tis of Thee. Then I got angry. Tried to live. Constitution. God's commandments. Then I crossed over and spoke with the enemy about all the lives taken. He could speak clear English and was void of hate. It was matter of fact between us. Then we came eye to eye and at the same time it was, "What do you want to do about it?". Then the Angel appeared.

No fear. Normal. Natural. We became a team under the influence of this directed to causal plane to retrieve others dying that day to reunite them with their loved ones. Then we, who agreed to stay, formed a 'band width' of some kind. That's why my family hasn't heard from me. Still got things to be and to do. Gone awhile. This will be no slow thing. As soon as Autumn comes, demeanor begins. Remember me by the three. Souls of Liberty are the Souls of Benghazi, a team guided and commanded by God, the Creator of the Whole Universe. Indeed, I may be able to walk right across the border again to be with mankind. (I would like that for you).

Star Spangled Banner
Taps – Loved that song. Eerie.
My Country Tis of Thee

And know that I AM the Constitution of the Constitution which is the 10 Commandments given by God to Moses. (I think this explains the power and the strength of His Grace that travels with him now to help the country and to help mankind. This Ty is truly a good man that can't be kept down)

Write them down Cathy for all to see, Taps has no true verse. It only has a story. I can hear it playing in my head. (Okay, do you mind if I add the Pledge of Allegiance?) Yes, changed much and very political. Others are not. (Okay).

The Star-Spangled Banner

O say can you see, by the dawn's early light,
What so proudly we hail'd at the twilight's last gleaming,
Whose broad stripes and bright stars through the perilous fight
O'er the ramparts we watch'd were so gallantly streaming?
And the rocket's red glare, the bombs bursting in air,
Gave proof through the night that our flag was still there,
O say does that star-spangled banner yet wave
O'er the land of the free and the home of the brave?

On the shore dimly seen through the mists of the deep
Where the foe's haughty host in dread silence reposes,
What is that which the breeze, o'er the towering steep,
As it fitfully blows, half conceals, half discloses?
Now it catches the gleam of the morning's first beam,
In full glory reflected now shines in the stream,
'Tis the star-spangled banner - O long may it wave
O'er the land of the free and the home of the brave!

And where is that band who so vauntingly swore,
That the havoc of war and the battle's confusion
A home and a Country should leave us no more?
Their blood has wash'd out their foul footstep's pollution.
No refuge could save the hireling and slave
From the terror of flight or the gloom of the grave,
And the star-spangled banner in triumph doth wave
O'er the land of the free and the home of the brave.

O thus be it ever when freemen shall stand
Between their lov'd home and the war's desolation!
Blest with vict'ry and peace may the heav'n rescued land
Praise the power that hath made and preserv'd us a nation!
Then conquer we must, when our cause it is just,
And this be our motto - "In God is our trust,"
And the star-spangled banner in triumph shall wave
O'er the land of the free and the home of the brave.

"Taps"

(some popular verses)

Day is done, gone the sun,
From the hills, from the lake,
From the sky.
All is well, safely rest,
God is nigh.

Go to sleep, peaceful sleep,
May the soldier or sailor,
God keep.
On the land or the deep,
Safe in sleep.

Love, good night, Must thou go,
When the day, And the night
Need thee so?
All is well. Speedeth all
To their rest.

Fades the light; And afar
Goeth day, And the stars
Shineth bright,
Fare thee well; Day has gone,
Night is on.

Thanks and praise, For our days,
'Neath the sun, Neath the stars,
'Neath the sky,
As we go, This we know,
God is nigh.

"America"

My country, 'tis of thee,
Sweet land of liberty,
Of thee I sing;
Land where my fathers died,
Land of the Pilgrims' Pride,
From every mountain side
Let freedom ring.

My native country, thee,
Land of the noble, free,
Thy name I love;
I love thy rocks and rills,
Thy woods and templed hills,
My heart with rapture thrills,
Like that above.

Let music swell the breeze,
And ring from all the trees
Sweet freedom's song;
Let mortal tongues awake,
Let all that breathe partake,
Let rocks their silence break,
The sound prolong.

Our fathers' God, to Thee,
Author of liberty,
To Thee we sing;
Long may our land be bright,
With freedom's holy light,
Protect us by Thy might,
Great God, our King.

THE TEN COMMANDMENTS OF GOD

1. I am the Lord thy God,
Thou shalt not have strange gods before me.

2. Thou shalt not take the name of the Lord thy God in vain.

3. Remember to keep holy the Sabbath day

4. Honor thy father and mother.

5. Thou shalt not kill.

6. Thou shalt not commit adultery.

7. Thou shalt not steal.

8. Thou shalt not bear false witness against thy neighbor.

9. Thou shalt not covet thy neighbor's wife.

10. Thou shalt not covet thy neighbor's (goods).

2 HOW I CAME TO CATHY

Be Still. Death is not what it used to be. You can now fight for the Land in which you loved = Earth. Many Aliens love Earth. Angels are part of our legion as it should be so it is. Heavens battle shall now be here. Yes, we still carry our stuff to work through. Still stuff to weed through, but just stuff, a realm, like evil, like witchcraft. Mother Teresa says. Say it again Cathy. (Mother Teresa says there is no time or energy to put into evil so do not. At least that is the basis of what she said that I can remember.) Correct give or take a bit.

First, a few messages for family. Where I am is love and it is uplifting. Wife, go on. Sad, but you knew.

Dad, see how all has become political and rage. Did your son die for nothing? Yes and no. I could have lived through that moment, but as God spoke and I looked up and saw with my own eyes, heart and head the reality of the Demon that was looking back at me through mankind, through a drone...(I am sorry, Sir, I lost it here) Others who crossed were watching the drone as I. We looked at each other in Spirit, eye upon eye and sank into the reality. We bonded into the trine in which Cathy sees. We were all on the same side after all. They loved their God and had their commitments too. It was all a set-up on both sides, equivalently. It was conniving.

We watched as others we knew or saw before death didn't go where we go. Surprised, amazed at the depth of difference between me and them.

Some I knew to be 'madmen' as friend, as co-worker in Spirit separated by the Divine in life equals enemies. By the Divine in life I meant that Evil inside. Hell has become as strong on Earth as it is in Heaven. People believe themselves which equals ego, which equals co-conspiracy with Hell and allows them to be non-directed by Heaven or humanity and therefore governed by the Spirit of Hell himself. The leader of the 'pack' was there with us then. But, I say, NO WAY to my Lord. The Divinity is in me to fight back, dead or not. That is when I saw the triangle of forces behind me and I joined as my body was broken. HE says to find Cathy. So I did. Blew her out of the water. (Yep, sure did). It's all good. Smooth now.

What Now?

(That 'what now?!' Is something we worked on for many, many months together. There are many conversations that are not written in this book because it was a testing time of friendship, loyalty, cleansing and clearing on both parts and a change in direction which brings us to 'What Now?')

First, let me reiterate that all souls are not lost now. Death equals awareness for those in battle. There is a sheath that has been lifted. Issues have been lifted and Grace granted by God. By issues, I mean worries, incompletions, 'karma' and so forth. It's time to get out your mojo! Some here on Earth will be asked to work with the trine. Others from the other side are joining by day and by night. We are growing in strength and working directly with mankind as if no 'crossing over' ever occurred. Do not deny the evidence of it. Do not deny your own direct intuition even if it doesn't make sense. LOVE WILL NOT FAIL. Not for country. Not for Man. Know that everyone is a 'tool' for something and for someone. I am a 'tool' for My God. MY GOD IS WITH ME. MY GOD IS WITH US.

We have Hell in the White House. Not speaking of people or individuals. Speaking of 'sway of spirit', 'sway of mind', as it was with Hitler, Mussolini, Rasputin and Christ's own Pontius Pilot. The world was consumed at that time. Must fight back against forces like 'entitlement' and 'thievery'. Even the Monks had to learn to fight to defend themselves against forces here on this Earth.

The curtain was shallower then than it is now, but on the brink of the same disorder unfolding. The 'new order' orchestrated by Satan cannot take over Earth without death and plague.

There is a new order ahead in Russia. Rasputin alive and well again in consciousness. In form not, but he has learned to bridge the gap between heaven and hell. Creator let him so he can truly die this time. (Ty, most people won't understand this. What do you want me to do?) Will call it as I see it. (Okay).

Evil hangs on. Sometimes it hangs on hard. Light just is. It's God. People, now is the time to come back to what it is in your life that evil distracts you from. Will be battling soon. Need all who are awake to make the conscious clearing to the soul. Prepare the young as now there are 'energy traps' that are hard to see and hard to feel. Battle is not about the skin but about the darkness within. Keep it clear. Smile. Laughter. Love within. Must be fearless. God will take care of the little things. One good deed for another goes a long way right now, however be warned of the need for the use of discernment as entitlement energy goes a long way in the disturbance of mankind. Take notice of the primary and secondary needs that are now being taken away from you and hoarded. It is never good when one claims they have the right to 'distribute your needs to you as they see fit'; all the while, taking twice as much back from you. And, watch out for those who say 'you work for me' or 'you exist for me' or 'I Rule you'.

Enjoy nature and freedom any way you can. Drink it in. Soon 'they' will be honing in on all your other freedoms like power, water, dwellings and so forth. Clear now for this cowardice. Obtaining extra finances will not carry you far enough in this. You must do the rest too. Align with others like you. Set the different ones free with grace. Can't do it for them anymore. Done for now.

(Another Day) War big. No defense, offense. No offense, defense. Liberate only half of specified nations Teams cross over, don't die, come here to Trine. What is happening here is that the gates of dimensions and areas in Heaven are being opened and prepared for a few things. The first of which is the Union of Spirit and Physical body, which will require a stretch of physics as we know it. It's like a broadening of the mind and awareness.

The next thing that is happening is that fallen warriors from across time are being united as one. All that is 'stuck' in them is being forgiven and they are being asked with utmost humbleness of Spirit to join the legions of Heaven in this Heavenly war which will inevitably have fall out on the nations of Earth. It is each individuals choice to join or not. If yes, they have a learning curve to go through once they are in the Trine energy encampment.

As the Trine is being gathered, so are individuals on Earth in order to complete the connection of energies and be compatible with Universal Law. You will be set in an intuitive learning curve accompanied by all above.

At the completion of this gathering and the completion of the 'training and aligning', there will be an increase in vibration of each individual and each as a collective whole. One mind. One body. One force. Six years it is taking place. All for now.

(Another Day) Collection of members of trine both alive and crossed over are in progress. You will know who you are and when and where you are to come. Use judgment skills all your own. Own up to no one . Use your gut. Use your intuition. Act as you will see the shots that need to be called here. It is not so important now to trim the physical body as it is to trim the MIND. Trim the EMOTIONS. Leave the past behind, with the exception of remembering history as a whole. Leave individual past behind. Think forward. Move forward. The past has happened how it has happened for the reasons it was meant to happen. Forgive it. Release it. Go on. Hate no one. Don't look back. Keep aiming forward towards the light and towards 'right' from 'wrong'. It's the only way to stay in form and not go crazy at this time.

I need to stress that there is no more 'gray area' in which to exist. No 'gray' in which to think, feel, live, compromise. The enemy is at hand and we as humans were/are only the tool to be discarded when the act is through, like bad sex. You have six years to complete this process in yourselves. Especially worried about
special forces in the military and otherwise. Time for council. Time for clean life and clean living. Keep cleaning life. Special note here. Lots of life can be cleansed with joy and laughter. Had to die to find that one out! Speaking of dying, it was no big deal. Creator made a better offer and you know how I love a good war – all puns intended. Hurts a little 'ripping' away the physical body, but it's okay. You do have to learn how to 'walk' again. Kind of like you can't feel your legs. Crossing over is a bit funny too because it's all 'peace and light'. Hard to accept. Had to move the personality over a bit and chill to receive it, but then the Angel started talking about war and truth and I realized he wasn't an 'ET', not that my gun worked anyway. Yes, I did try. Can't believe I tried to shoot God. Oh well. Was a good laugh in the end for all of us.

They removed me from physical to Spirit really fast. Turns out that most guys shape up in the physical mirror for 10 days running back and forth checking on everyone and seeing things they couldn't see before. Some are still haunted and floating out there somewhere between right and wrong and exploring other planets. I am trying to call them back now. Need your help to call all those lost in Spirit who are warriors back in time to the call of Spirit. You have worked and suffered enough. Come and fight the good fight now.

Creating a 'magnet'; generating a grand white light for them to see and sending the message that they are worthy. Suffering is over. All they have to do is to lean ever so slightly to the Trine. We, their friends, buddies will do the rest to call them back.

Need you who are alive to help. Any and every fallen warrior you know or have known in any way, shape or form needs you to call on them to go to this heavenly light. I don't care if it's just someone that grabbed your heart from the newspaper. I was directed to Cathy and she was directed to me. Pray. Pray like there is no tomorrow for these lost souls because if they are left alone they will fall prey to the great unknown for an eternity. I won't stop until the job is done and neither will Cathy and all of you who are called. This is our job. This is our mission.

When it is done (The Trine complete) in Heaven, we will gather you all on Earth in your own individual and unique expressions and we will battle together.

Angels getting to know. I'm still working on that one. Strange, I can run right through them. Yep, tried the charge in the beginning too. They are outside the Trine, yet in the Trine at the same time. (Why are you called Trine?) Don't know. Just is a statement of fact. We all just knew it to be the Trine. We all just knew the Angels on High that were there surrounding, guiding and directing. We all just knew each other. I just knew you.

3 THE ANGELS SPEAK

WE WILL DANCE THROUGH THIS FIRE.

Respect your animal kingdom. Respect the wind, the air you breathe, the trees, stones, stars and the vibration of the seas. Ask, don't command of them. Allow the FREE WILL of their souls to come into the Trine as we allowed you to come in. They are extraordinarily damaged as a result of the damaged child of God we call Satan today. To us he is nothing more than 'unruly child'. Fear not. Although spanking will not be enough for evil truly does abide in him. That is why it is our fight. (I don't understand why man then. Why the Trine?)

Yes, it is we who organized and operate the Trine as per His order and Divine instruction. All tribes under this sacred and Divine union are rewarded like no other since the beginning of time. This 'spoiled teenager', as Jesus calls him is aligned more perfectly to his own destruction than you know. In order to fight with mankind, he had to agree to it. Although he did not need to carry, take it as far as he did. Hate so strongly, but truly loves his own. Confused individual race of Beings, but Beings non the less under the domain of the Maker Himself. Stop being foolish, Him, Her, makes no difference to us. (Sorry, my mind trailed off into the fight that so often occurs these days about the domain of God being man or woman. I was just thinking of how blind and stupid we've become to let such silly distractions blind us and stop us in our tracks. Humor me, please, WASHINGTON REDSKINS, Hoorah!) Okay! Feel better? Good, let's go on. Funny to us to the conniving ways unruly child uses to obtain less freedom for man. He thinks we never completed the mind of Man, but we did. Underground until this time. This is why we need man. Awakening other centers of the brain fire not in use until this time. Guided framework of Existence. Trine completes aspects of Courage, Fight or Flight, Trauma, Drama, Weakness, Confinement, Limitation and Freedom to Act and Obtain Creator here on Earth.

Let us go back, back in time to a faraway place for most of man to conceive. Cathy, you know Atlantis was organized in Heaven and brought down to the Earth. You were there twice, although you only remember once. You were the old man too who came back to follow and guide you as the child you spoke of in the other book (Walking With Angels).

It was I, Michael, your uncle, who made you free that day. (I, affectionately named Archangel Michael 'Uncle' eons ago) I brought, commanded the wind and the fires of the sea to save thee. Now it is I who must free thee again and free the creatures of the seas, the lands and the fires on the wind. Was truly a Wicked day.

My heart sank as did yours. We knew man to be FREE of suffering and at Liberty to go beyond the limitations and extensions you see today. I held you tight. I held you close. I wrapped you around me as a scarf while you held the sea and allowed all to be free. You decided to allow all to 'run' to seek refuge in order to be free. You've felt guilty for this ever since. You could not have saved man that day. Suffer not, you see it is a far reach, but can you see that in retreat you gathered strength? Can you not see that you put everything in a 'void' to be able to see on the Earth what you see today. That would be the lands, the trees and the others you called to your aid. Even the Salt of the Sea.

You see, you were standing there trying to free the sanctity of it all by yourself. Although the air we breathe is free, the lands, the seas, the destruction is not. Our world, your world has been simply waiting to be freed. The Trine contains all who were in that space and time since the beginning of Creation two fold. Remember, *Physical Bodies, were made at that time. The creation of the Earth made freedom for the mold of the physical structure only. Before that you were with Me.*

All bodies, all souls, all beings from elsewhere and including the lands, the trees and the seas were hated by him then – unruly child. He, before he came here had already reached beyond the dimensions and untruthfully saying and making 'angels' of these predecessors of mankind. He claimed them to be freer and above man in His eyes. He claimed to be diplomat of me and of Him. Had power to make them 'angels' but not without disruption of mind and thinking and not without destruction of figuring mathematical equation for seeing. Hence, figures we call Demon.

No need to be free of a Demon. Fear not. Only a conduit of his evil presence, but an equal being to thee non the less. He, the Demon needs to be freed of unruly child too. Alas, some major damage has been done to them as well. Will have quite a job returning them to their own unity. Will probably at this point be to their own destruction of themselves. So, fear not, when they confront you from within even the sanctity of 'safe' places. Spirit, Divine, Trine is with you from here on out.

Suffer no more the needy, entitlement or the violent. Their destruction is their own. The mind is annoying and ignoring their direct calling from all species of Heaven to correct their modes of being and come into the light before being eaten alive at death from the embodiment of what consumes them.

Aging was not meant to be present. That was not a Creator force or wisdom. That came and comes from indistinct interpretations of unruly child and his kingdom. Yes, his Father granted him a kingdom to his own destruction.

Entitlement mentality whether it be emotional, anger or fear based was not a Creator force or interpretation. That was a malfunction and an evil desire from unruly child. Made him laugh to see people beg, command and against one another. That was what you saw him doing that day. You were calm. You were collected. You were helpful and commanding of all the forces at your hands and completion to do before I saved you. We, the Archangels, were enraged in battle with HIM in Heaven at the time as you all – all Beings of Light in Atlantis 'held the fort down' with all your might until We came. Atlantis was not complete. Man was not complete. Earth was young and perhaps a little raw in its distinction. One cannot do it all. Requires a force in the beginning, the middle and the end.

Yes, it is I, Michael who commands the force as I commanded Israel. The United States is an indefinite extension and force of Israel in Heaven.

Truly no nation is against another in the sight of God. It is in the eyes of this wisdom that the Trine must unite. Forces of Evil are behind destruction. But you know that. Fear not. Your physical body will catch up after all these years of writing, channeling and speaking with us. You forget sometimes that it is only one Angel full of Evil at the head of their fight. You are beside me and a legion of much stronger Angels than he. Try, try to see the forest for the trees. The Trine will begin soon to help the union of mankind stretch and see beyond the sheath that he, unruly child placed upon all of thee. The beginning of time was three, not what you see in the apple. (Adam and Eve).

First you were brought here before me after the desire of Creator. Then you were brought upon the energetic playground in which you see, Heaven. Then we, as a collective whole, prayed in unity the design that came to be which was breathed into by His Divine Image.

It was only after that the Earth was designed in order to be free to be. Physical vehicle reality. All souls agreed to be here even after the destruction. Choice. Time. All asked. All agreed.

Some will give up and give in, but it is only out of seduction and curiosity to know 'what unruly child's deal is'.

Yes, there are some that are already destroyed. Do not worry. Compassion in Heaven. Please, Catherine, focus simply on me. I will complete thee. I will do the rest. (Okay. What about all those who are engrossed in unruly child's domain along with the Demons? What about those who truly 'like it'?)

Entitlement, Angry, Emotionally distraught. Yes, suicide falls in these categories. One third will come over to the Trine. They will wake up and not fall. Two thirds are numb and dumb, nothing more than food for the weary spirits of Satonic issue. They will be eaten alive, used for food, no life left. No soul left. They will not suffer in Heaven for their seduction, their breech comes only from Satan himself, unruly child.

It will, however take a millennium to recover from the sacrifice of their own souls. One thing is certain. These souls will never give up power over themselves again. Do you see now where those types of battles are best left to Heaven and to His Divine Guidance.

Disturb it not on the planet anymore. Too much time wasted on 'Psychology' of suffering. That always was and is God's. Pray for it. Manage it via Prayer. End your suffering of it, otherwise become taken in by the wave of destruction in the 'sea' of unruly child.

Now is the time for all to turn inward and up. Put the oxygen mask on yourself first before you can gear up to help another.

Yes, we will be appearing more, as will Demons and Ghosts. You see, those who are stuck suffer too in those realms. They are now being freed and given free will to continue to surrender to unruly child or to go beyond their own belief systems and expectations to join forces here or there.

Follow your heart Cathy. I know your heart is with Him. Follow your heart and your heart will follow you. Continue to be free. (I ask you to help me and I allow my Self to open up much more on all levels at this time to assist Ty and to assist the Trine. It is my path, my duty, my call to help) And so it is. So Be It Catherine Ferrier Smith. All for now.

(Ty, I wish you were still alive) He is Alive. Feel him breathe. Use your senses. Feel him breathe and you will see that you can touch him. Veil being lifted between death and the physical. Allows him to appear, although sometimes suddenly he has to aspirate. He is learning too.

(I know we as humans need to be aware , be prepared and align with the Almighty Presence to the best of our ability and stay close to the Trine. What else do we do?) Recognize distractions and even though you are committed to mankind suffer not the humiliation in your heads of being dedicated to things, people, situations that are needy and distracting of your true calling. Remove guilt of claiming time for self. Get what you intuit needs to be done, done. Know that all will align with relationships, friends, colleagues at another place and time.

Waste no more time justifying your existence to politicians. If it's a bad employee, get rid of it. Your obligation now is to proceed, to succeed, to prosper, be healthy, wealthy and young. Your obligation is to turn to your God first inside each and every one of you. Nation and family next, equally and, finally, your atmosphere, the lands and the seas.

Tend to that like a farmer tends to his crops. HE is not speaking of 'going green'. HE is speaking of honoring the life that exists in all things.

It is a foolish belief system to remain entitled in anything or situation. Do all you can do to release that from your existence. Keep prayer. Yes, we know how you feel about the idiocracy in the governments, both local and abroad. Greed, power, inability to grasp the Divine Truth about their actions affecting the future.........stop. Let it go. Give it to God and follow your gut instincts. Is not your current government part of 'entitlement energy' around you. If you know about it, it is you. Change it completely.

Increase your awareness. Increase your skill in whatever it is that you do. Remain connected to the Earth so that you may survive this energetic strife coming to you. Love, but don't lean so hard as to push the other down.

You know your right from your left. Well now is the time to know your right from your wrong when it comes to Universal Law and Physics.

It's time to live completely in right from wrong in the Earth plane. No more compromise. Must choose. Will be most difficult at times. Your answers must be your own between you and your Creator – not owning up to man or mankind or things as they 'should be'. Be your own breeze. Sing your songs that you are attracted to beyond belief systems as the ideology of our patriot belief system songs. Songs that move you into prayer. Songs that move you like a prayer.

There is a need for discrepancy in words. Use words combined with the bodies of the body wisely. For 'politically correct' is an image, not an idea. Do you understand what we mean? An idea can represent a state of Being, of existence. Does one, do you truly desire to live and exist in an image? You as a people are all designed with Him and His grace in mind. Large, small, short, tall big, thin, black, brown, brunette or blond all happen, all exist at the same time for the finery of HIS IMAGE, HIS IDEA, like a fine thread woven into existence. A fine balance as you are. Changing image for desire of health or wealth of mind is one thing, creating your physical being and existence because of a 'mindset' and an image of another's desire will certainly burn you up in the fire and crush you.

Own what you are as a vehicle. Do what you enjoy. Be serious about that. If you can do that, the rest of the field (parts of the body, mind and soul) will realize that much of what it carries is 'so what', therefore giving less fuel for the negative, destructive forces to enter and/or to speak to you. Will also make you lighter, freer, faster for the Trine to work with you and for those in His command to enter upon you in the physical.

Do the same for aging. Fear not aging when there is a legion of His Army beside and behind you. Strength like you've never seen before!

We love you all. We are a lot alike mankind and I AM. And, we both committed long ago to follow in His Image and in His Path.

Lean not on the commitments of others to His Commandments or His commands. Honor all religions at this time. Honor ALL.

Continue to look up for your allies and your connections for War. You are children and squabbles will always be predominant as you play where you are, so see beyond (Earth plane existence and mentality). Look up. Join together as adults in Spirit.

(Ty now) Time is lost. Have to go back to work. See you later. We all have to go now. Complete.

4 OTHERS SPEAK?

When you walk to the edge of all the light you have,
and take that first step into the darkness of the
unknown, you must believe that one of two things will
happen: There will be something solid for you to stand
upon, or, you will be taught how to fly."
--Patrick Overton

Our Boys, Our Trine are taught how to FLY, and fly they will to aid
in the war between Heaven and Hell.

Stand aside, Satan, or whoever or whatever you are. We are in the
mightiness of our one union and of our Father above. You cannot
separate us now – not in consciousness, not in body, not in soul,
not in mind. We exist, therefore we ARE the I AM and not you,
anyone or anything can take that away from us ever again.

(The others speak to me now, Russian, American, European,
Australian and some from the East) All suffering is complete. We
got it out of our system (The Japanese and the Africans are
approaching now. Middle Eastern were still kneeling in prayer
before they could/would discuss with me. The Middle East take a
longer time to get to know). We no longer carry the pain of our old
wars, only the experience and the know-how. It is a Greatness to
Be of the Light at this time. We all want our Beloved in Mankind
to know our suffering has ended and so will theirs. (Now enter all
nations of POW, MIA and Killed in Action, but left alive to
remember for the rest of the lifetime = much psychological,
emotional and energetic damage. Now enter in 'street people' and
'woodsmen' who left their societies due to depression and let their
lost years slip by) We are gaining in strength. (They all look, feel
happy and strong) Want to tell our loved ones on the planet at this
time the gifts we gave them long ago, we will give them again. We
will win. We are no longer under the guise of another's political
rage. We join because we want to. We suffer not the duality of
suggestion and seduction, i.e., being bent to another's will. We did
not have to be talked into anything. The angels did not disguise

themselves. They laid their cards out on the table and blocked not the truth or their surroundings. This is their fight and they indeed asked for our help. Build a bridge, so to speak. It was our own decision first, then we found out our gifts in return for our work. But, to be honest, we are all doing what we were born to do as you who are called from the Earth plane of existence to join us at this time. This, we agree is a true 'calling'.

(Those who were slaves from all nations step up, as do those from the Middle East) We prefer to work directly with Spirit. We fear that mankind will ruin things as they have done in the past, but HE won't do it without you so we must come. Plagues are to be of a concern. Mystics and players of energy destroy what is before them to destroy. Chemicals abound. Misery can come. Be aware Catherine Smith. Ten percent of what comes from the government to the people is true. Need to decipher the rest. Put their conversations, their 'announcements' together, three or four at a time in order to eak out forty percent of the truth. The rest you must figure out, intuit, for yourselves. It is imperative that you gather with those of like minds. Not to say one is right or one is wrong, but the safety net is in not belonging to the Gray organization. There is no 'compromise'. You are either black or you are white. It is as simple as all that.

Your government and others let an oil well spill for days and then for weeks just to achieve some sort of 'power' and announcement to the rest of the world. Stay away from those who speak of power in that manner. Stay away from minds that state that 'Medics' are needed and they are really their security guards. Stay away. That is all we can tell you at this time. Pray that the things mankind has to suffer at this point simply go away. Do not worry about trying to 'turn it into something else'. Let Creator take that away and do it for you. Yours is one nation under God. So is ours. It is a 'New World Order'. But that new world order is of Christ the Lord, not Satan, the one-unit bank. Poverty was not meant to be. Close now.

(The next day) We are not worker bees. We are not ants. We are all of separate, individual powers and minds, yet we are complete as a collective whole. We think and act as our own mind and as a whole. Close now.

(And, the next day, another speaks) Random multipliers of success speaks to the nation of wise moments and wise movements. Battle is in heaven, not with men. Repeat, battle is in heaven, not with men. Leave theses human beasts alone. Go out of the realm of men. Prayer is deeper in the East than in the west. Formulate your avenues there. Under one Being. Under one creative force with all of mankind and beyond. Lay down your metal sword. Pick up your spiritual sword. Allow that Divinity to guide and construct your path. No longer the path of others. No longer the path of ancestry. Ancestry being used to destroy at this time. Will come back again. Able bodied men dying out there supposed to be of creative forces of the Divine, but are not. Are being slaughtered by bastardy of higher forces being used to influence mankind behind an iron curtain of 'promised democracy' of all lands, of all beings. But will not be that way. Trap as sand is a pit to fall in and sink into the abyss. That is all this force can truly promise. Has had the last two hundred years to formulate jealousy. Commitment is to rage, violence and destroying human life. I never truly believed the creature exists. But he does exist and he does formulate armies against mankind. Right now he aids in the military, mental and
psychological destruction of mankind. Must stop our armies from using forces not divided into unity in our being. NOT REASON, NOT DEMAND, but a polluted desire to STINK UP THE VESSEL of ALL of mankind – every man, woman and child so that they may never reach up and advance again to the Divine Kingdom. Never again to receive the Divine Grace that He holds for each and every one of us. That is our mission. Mankind. We unite to formulate all the desires of man; all the truths and formats to see what He sees a branch, so to speak to see what He sees and light the space between what guides us and what destroys us. We unite in space and time. Conflicts resolved. Trust issues going away. Angels go in between and unite us, our garbage I think. So, we are a Trine of Free Energy Beings, forgiven of all of our Earthly wounds and display of egotistical and justifiable denial. We speak the truth united as a force. We believe the truth united as a force of His Kingdom. We act out desires of His Kingdom here on Earth with Man. Better than day job.

31

(That makes me laugh as he shows me that in one instant while alive he is full of hatred and screaming to kill; angry that he had walked into the path of the bright blond American, the other Seal and feeling the pain ring through his body expecting to 'wrench' forth onto the ground, only to be received by a great Angelic Being in the light in the next instant who set him down to assign him his new path. He can see 30 or 40 more who are with him sitting down and being talked to, all in chairs, all in Divine confusion and shock. Then a great light came down toward them and they received grace and 'ruptures of life' are taken away. They are armed somehow and set to duty. He tells me that I know that great light as Michael and that Ty is set to lead. He is a good man. This man is second in the lead, but still hates to talk to women, so he won't tell me his name as he wants something of life to hold on to. Then he laughs and gently grabs my chin, which feels like a very fond gesture as he leads me back into the Trine to show me around. Somehow, his ugliness needed to earn my trust as I needed to earn his. Ty just knew all about me.)

(I am getting a picture of groups of men, angels and other worldly beings are gathered in an encampment in the light. It feels like day. Nothing matters here about day or night, food, anything. It feels like a captive void that all agree to. Can't feel the joy, but I can feel the light. And, I can feel a great many energies holding the light. As they pass each person/being, the person/being smiles again and brightens this man who leads me now tells me his name is Russo. Russo says that these are the latest Russians who came to join. I see members of the animal kingdom there as well. Then I notice Ty is behind me. Takes my hand to take the lead)

Did you not think the Earth is to a great degree, dedicated to man? To a great degree, all are with us now. All except Ambassador. Confused being. Had to agree to go somewhere else to heal. Very psychologically shaken at degree of death. Frozen. Needs to thaw. Others just weren't sure if they wanted to join us as they preferred to do other, more joyous things first. Needed to heal that in order to come on board. All here now.

Here we practice all day uniting with the Lord and all night seeing the disease and destruction and the path that needs to be made. This is where you come in. You cannot live here or stay with us, but I can and do bind your path to my own. Kneel beside me here. Free yourself from your wide degree of worries. Leave them right here for Creator to see. (It is now that I realize that Ty uses the vibration of the word 'Creator' so as to speak genuinely and kindly to all who come here who still have personalities and their own private connections to the Divine. He respects and initiates in this way.) It is my job to nurse maid these ingrates back to health so that they can speak their own language but be free to be with me and bind this hatred that this creature hides behind in everything he sees. It is my job to unbind man at this time. It is time for the path way to be carved for all my brothers to join forces here directly as they cross over into the light, forgiven of all daily sins. Repeat, forgiven of all daily sins. Unite and fight the good fight here and now with respect to the unity of mankind, not the division or the 'spoils'. We had it before we will create it again.

Kneel here and pray. Right here. Will receive you again and get you, lead the way out of here.

(10 minutes go by and I realize that I am feeling the funny way I feel here because my place is on Earth. Must cleanse and clear body with water and keep mind in the light. I also realize that this is the book's end. This is an energy platform of united beings, of which I am somehow a part of. This 'platform' of energy is compassing its way through the Earth.) From this point forward, stay alert. Don't deny your own energy. Listen to the inquiry of Spirit. Connect and follow the lead that will be held 'in the gut', so to speak. Don't panic. Give craziness, worry and fear back to God on a daily basis and follow your feet. Ask all the world to do the same. Alert that this Trine will be passionately speaking to mankind as will the Angels that guide it. Satan will not rule this time.

It is true that the times are about to get crazier, but the thing to do is to stay wide, keeping your energy field clean and clear, abiding in truth and keeping no regrets. Keep praying. This war is guided by and belongs to the Angels and these distant forces. Follow their lead that will be loud like dynamite exploding in your head. Keep true to your visions. Know that you can help Man at this time, but what is united or controlled by other forces must stay there to be 'safe' at this point. The angels tell me now that ALL MEN will be saved. Not a degree will be lost to this thing. Some may take lifetimes to heal and turn around, but turn around they will. Some are being held in strange destinies in order to advance and go forward and some need to know the Beast in order to go forward.

Cannot judge. Nor will you even be able to discriminate. You can only keep your own and those which intuition guides you to.

The sole purpose of this writing is to make aware that Mankind is a vision that God SEES. Even though you are purposefully being brought in to a war, you will ultimately be being led back to Him with much Grace from this point forward. Stay awake. Stay aware. Do all that you can do to maintain your physical vehicles in the light. Repair your Nations. Repair your Nations. Repair your Nations.

You were born in the light. You will stay in the light. Let the confused and the drama be what it is BESIDE you, not in you. Intuition will do the rest.

(Ty stands behind me now.) Cathy it will be alright. It's like a butterfly. You will be like a butterfly. Stay close. Stay behind his light, guarded, guided and directed.

Tell my family to Laugh. Even though I will be light, I will be with them. I will be there to show them the light of day. I have a lot of sisters! (Laughs. Leads me out of the Trine and back to where I began.)

(But, before he leaves, he shows me a wooden throne and then I see Satan going to sit in it). He built it here. God didn't give it to him here. He is allowed here because he is a son of God, but he was not granted here. He is all wrapped up in his own soul. Half the time he doesn't even know we are here watching, serving the Lord by keeping an eye on things. (I feel so uncomfortable being anywhere near this beast). We will have to face him. We will have to fight, you and me. (So, I embrace the uncomfortable feeling like 'taking a bull by the horns'. I vow to release all resistance and control right now in my own being and prepare to be what Creator needs me to be for this union between He and Mankind. Won't work unless I can work it for me. Otherwise I'll be useless for all three, the Father, the Son and the Holy and Divine Spirit. Something happens to me as I feel something heavy lift from me, the beast turns around to see me as my 'lightness' is now on. I have no fear or resistance as I realize that he can't come near me because I am free and of the light. Ty is holding my hand tight.)

(There are others of this Trine who desire to speak and all have directly the same sentiments as Ty, Russo and the Angels. There are many there from distant places and times.)

(Ty heads up all the POWS, MIA, Retired and Active Alive Military who unite. I can see thousands and thousands more from all over Europe as well as USA who join the United Band, as it is now called, since I began working with Ty. He is a grand and fine leader for this crusade. There are those who truly do cross over to be of higher service from the other side.)

(Ty reminds me that there are those who are Divine on what he now calls 'the other side' who conceive treasures he never had in life that some deceased may never have.) Good to Live, isn't it Cathy. You are young, wise. Be free to standardize, unite His Holy Kingdom. More to come than you may realize. All for now. Close the book.

About the Author

Catherine was inspired to travel to Beijing because her father and greatest inspiration, Jack Ferrier, was one of the first Americans to be allowed back into China in the 1970's. Jack Ferrier was an extraordinarily gifted photographer and movie director in the military. He was on President Nixon's and Henry Kissinger's personal staff. Jack Ferrier is a Vietnam War Veteran and prior to being on the presidential staff, he was a top gun for the first Apollo missions to the moon. He never stopped! After the Nixon Administration he continued to direct and produce all kinds of training films for the Navy and taught the Alaska Area Natives how to use closed-circuit TV so they could run it in their own hospitals. Catherine learned truths about many men and many cultures through her father. He taught her to hold herself to herself, use her abilities, pay attention, and be strong and as fearless as possible and to persevere. In fact, because of her strength, she was one of the Americans brought up to stand before the younger Chinese people as a symbol of where they as a people desired to go in the future during the so-called uprising at Tian an Men Square in Beijing. Having to rely on her Psychic abilities, rather than knowing the Mandarin language, she was able to connect, communicate and go into and out of a particular situation. She passes her methods on.

In Beijing, in addition to finely tuning her Psychic abilities, she worked and trained in the Guang an Men Hospital, Xi Yuan Hospital and at the China National Research Institute of Sports Science. She has experience in Energy Healing with extreme arthritic patients, paraplegics, infants, pregnancy, headaches, PMS, colds, flu, cancer, trauma recovery from and preparation for surgery, broken bones/sprains/strains, lymphatic drainage,

reflexology, depression, detoxification, relaxation, stress, constipation, colon hydrotherapy, back walking and sports injury. In fact, these studies brought Catherine to author her second book, "Holistic Healing; Age Reversal and Body Rejuvenation Made Easy!"

Since Catherine, is a naturally gifted Psychic and a naturally gifted "Hand's On Healer" and was in China, she added training in sports therapy, back walking, bone setting and therapy needles on some of China's Olympic teams (the fencing, wrestling, swimming and gymnastics teams). Both traditional (eastern) and western methods were applied. While training in hand's on practices, she donated her time giving Psychic Readings, assisted by a translator, to the doctors and families. She truly got to know and to experience on a first hand level, lifestyle and thought processes which added dimensions to her Life Coaching abilities!

In 1997 and 1998 Catherine continued her studies of Psychic and Energy Healing in Manila and LaUnion Philippines at the Philippine Spiritual Help Foundation with Psychic Healer, Rev. Alex Orbito. While in the Philippines working with Mr. Orbito, she fine-tuned her abilities to communicate with Angels, Animals, Nature, Extraterrestrials, and assist people to their Akashic Records and speak to those Loved Ones who have crossed over.

Catherine continued her energy studies in Europe, Mexico and Canada as well as here in the United States on both the East and West Coasts. In Canada, Mexico and Europe, she focused on more finely tuning her Psychic Abilities as an Intuitive Life Coach which brought her to author her first book; "Self Life Coaching; 21 Days That Will Transform Your World!"

Catherine never ceases to be open to her psychic abilities. She is forever excited about Life and all aspects of it! She recognizes the need for healing of all levels, including by "traditional" means, and promotes and supports healing and healers of all types. The Psychic Energy Realm knows no bounds!

"If only one would take the time to get to know the Self, one would realize that the Self is eager to assist always and in all ways"

- Catherine Ferrier (Smith)

Current Activities, Schools and Information

Catherine currently hosts a global LIVE Talk Radio Show entitled 'Let's Talk Paranormal!' You can see archived shows on www.BBMGlobalNetwork.com and on www.Spreaker.com.

Catherine works directly with Post Traumatic Stress Syndrome of all kinds for people of all ages, but especially with our war veterans and wounded warriors and their families.

Catherine owns an online Reiki School and has an Online Paranormal School in the works. Her world travels have brought her to connect with a Paranormal Healing Team therefore covering all the Self Help, Spiritual Healing and Life Coaching aspects. Not to mention, covering all of your Paranormal Investigation needs!

Catherine constantly channels information from the angels and from the other side. People from all walks of life constantly request that Catherine retrieve messages from their Loved Ones who have crossed over. And an even greater number of people ask

for assistance with those who may be possessed or have dwellings that are possessed with negativity.

Yet, another level of channeling information comes through Catherine with speaking to Beings from other worlds. She has been able to help a great deal with those who have experienced all paranormal situations from Alien abduction to speaking to other planetary beings such as the Pleadians, vampires, ghosts and more.

Go to www.AHealingLifeCoach.com for more information. Schedule a phone, internet or email session.

Other Channeled /Researched Books by Catherine Ferrier

"Self-Life Coaching; 21 Days That Will Transform Your World!"

"Holistic Healing; Age Reversal and Body Rejuvenation Made Easy!"

"Walking With Angels"

Contact Information:

www.AHealingLifeCoach.com

Catherine_Ferrier_Smith@yahoo.com

www.ingramcontent.com/pod-product-compliance
Lightning Source LLC
Chambersburg PA
CBHW030549290526
45786CB00004B/1943